Dedicated to Izzy and Carter. Be brave, kind, and work hard.
And always, be yourself.

Big Sur

By Alysson Foti Bourque

ISBN-13:978-0692660737
ISBN-10:0692660739

Published by
Alysson Foti Bourque / ICAD
alyssonbourque@yahoo.com
337.316.0813

On the horizon our journey begins, a tree grows tall at the mountain's bend.

Trails winding as far as you stop, all from the view from the chimney's top.

Nature's sun grows fresh from the ground, blowing
quietly without a sound.

Alone in the nest from a day so serene, camouflaged ten feet high, not to be seen.

A house carved out of the mountain pass, secure on the Pacific for moments to last.

Outside of the redwoods, adventures lie, sailing the bay as whales swim by.

Sea lions applaud as you sail towards the sun, your obstacles are left on Highway One.

Rolling hills on the edge of blue, stand so high where no one can see you.

The timber of a redwood is the effort you hold dear, if there lies no resistance, no one can hear.

Retreat in your path after the mist clears the boundaries,
let the nature reside right where you found me.

Rocks line the bank, to guard the bay, the water always crashing on a hot July day.

Back at your ranch, greeted by turkeys who feed, just nature so great is all you need.

Shades of sunset mark a day so full, memories created from an endless pool.

In the shadows of the curvy unknown, adventures are coming and curiosity has grown.

A sun so bright in a clear, crisp sky, shine the wave of the flowers to a near passerby.

Trails to hike as far as far wide, greeted by the vast oceanside.

Where the water takes you, is where the story ends,
only thing left is a postcard to send.

Goodbye Big Sur, until our next journey, see you soon, please don't forget me.

The End

About the Author

Alysson Foti Bourque is the author of the book series, Rhyme or Reason Travels. This series takes children and adults on an abstract journey through the world's most spectacular wonders. The concise rhyme and figurative art allows readers of all ages to provide their emotions and interpretations of shapes and color to inspire the individual's cognitive creativity. Alysson received a degree in elementary education from the University of Louisiana at Lafayette, a law degree from Southern University Law Center, and currently receives inspiration for her work through motherhood. Alysson is currently working on her new children's picture book series based on a witty feline character, Alycat, with a larger than life personality as she makes her daydreams become reality. Stayed tuned for more on the Alycat series.

www.ingramcontent.com/pod-product-compliance
Lightning Source LLC
Chambersburg PA
CBHW041243040426
42445CB00004B/132